About Mastering Basic Skills—"Real-Life" Math Word Problems:

Welcome to Rainbow Bridge Publishing's Mastering Basic Skills—"Real-Life" Math Word Problems series. Students often ask their parents and teachers, "When am I ever going to use this?" Mastering Basic Skills "Real-Life" Math Word Problems has been developed to help students see the many uses of math in the world around them. The word problems in this book help students develop problem-solving skills in real-world situations while increasing confidence in their math skills.

Content for this book is based on current NCTM (National Council of Teachers of Mathematics) standards and supports what teachers are currently using in their classrooms. Word Problems can be used both at school and at home to engage students in problem solving.

The third-grade math skills used in this book include addition, subtraction, multiplication, division, graphing, fractions, measurement, money values, and time.

Table of Contents

© Rainbow Bridge Publishing   www.summerbridgeactivities.com

Fishy Facts

Name _____   Date _____

◇ Start Here!

Solve each problem. The first problem is worked for you.

1 Keshia has 37 goldfish in her aquarium. Mark has 19 in his aquarium. How many more goldfish does Keshia have than Mark?

$$\begin{array}{r} {\scriptstyle 21} \\ \cancel{37} \\ -\ 19 \\ \hline \textbf{18 goldfish} \end{array}$$

2 Jake has 58 guppies and 84 goldfish. How many fewer guppies than goldfish does Jake have?

3 Ben has 47 more goldfish than Leslie. Leslie has 73. How many goldfish does Ben have?

4 Isabel's aquarium has 43 plants. She took out 29 plants. How many plants does Isabel have left in her aquarium?

5 Jamal's friend gave him 17 goldfish. He had 69 to start with. How many does he have now?

6 Denise has 93 comets in her aquarium. Jack has 35 comets in his aquarium. How many more comets does Denise have than Jack?

7 Marcus has 25 guppies in his aquarium. Lucy has 17 more guppies than Marcus has. How many guppies does Lucy have?

Did you know?

Fish have no eyelids. When you turn on the lights in a room, goldfish will swim for cover. They can't block out the light, so they will look for shelter among plants. Although goldfish can't close their eyes, they do sleep!

Name _____   Date _____

◇ Start Here!

Make up numbers to solve each problem. The first problem is worked for you.

1   Paige sees <u>28</u> tourists with cameras and <u>29</u> tourists with binoculars. There are 57 tourists altogether.

$$\begin{array}{r} \overset{1}{2}8 \\ +\ 29 \\ \hline 57 \end{array}$$

2   Ginger has ___ postcards. She mails ___ postcards. Now Ginger has 38 postcards left.

3   Mario drove ___ miles on Wednesday. On Thursday Jack drove ___ miles. Jack and Mario drove 97 miles altogether.

4   Jackson bought ___ souvenirs. His little sister broke ___ of the souvenirs. Jackson has 46 souvenirs left.

5   On Friday, Hector sells ___ maps to the movie stars' homes. Saturday, Hector sells ___ maps. Hector sells 82 maps in all.

6   Caroline buys a poster from every city she visits. On her first trip she buys ___ posters. On her second trip she buys ___ posters. She now has 57 posters.

7   Emily drives a tour bus. She drives ___ tourists to the beach and ___ tourists to the canyon. In all, Emily drives 74 tourists to the beach or the canyon.

8   Caleb works in a hotel. He has ___ pieces of luggage to put in the rooms. He drops off ___ pieces of luggage on the 21st floor. He has 51 pieces of luggage left.

Weather Highs and Lows

Name _____   Date _____

◇ Start Here!

Solve each problem. The first problem is worked for you.

1 The highest temperature in Duluth, Minnesota, was 97° F. The highest temperature in Barrow, Alaska, was 79° F. How much warmer was Duluth than Barrow?

$$\begin{array}{r} \overset{8\,1}{\cancel{9}7}° \\ -\ 79° \\ \hline 18°\ \text{warmer} \end{array}$$

2 Seattle, Washington, received 37 inches of rain in a year. Jackson, Mississippi, had 55 inches of rain. How much more rain did Jackson get than Seattle?

3 The maximum normal temperature in January for Houston, Texas, is 61° F. Rapid City, South Dakota, has a maximum normal temperature of 34° F in January. How much colder is Rapid City than Houston?

4 The weather station in Baltimore, Maryland, reported its fastest wind at 41 miles per hour. Fairbanks, Alaska, reported its fastest wind at 26 miles per hour. How much faster was the wind that was reported in Baltimore?

5 In July, the highest temperature in Los Angeles, California, was 84° F. The lowest temperature during the same month was 65° F. What was the difference between the highest and lowest temperature?

Did you know?

The hottest temperature recorded in the United States was 134° F in Death Valley, California, on July 10, 1913.

The coldest temperature recorded in the United States was -80° F at Prospect Creek, Alaska, January 23, 1971.

Movie Mania

Name _____ Date_____

◇ Start Here!

Solve each problem. The first problem is worked for you.

1 Alexis sold 1,223 cups of Fizzy Cola. Sam sold 873 cups. How many cups of Fizzy Cola did Alexis and Sam sell altogether?

$$\begin{array}{r} \overset{1}{1,223} \\ +\ \ 873 \\ \hline 2,096 \text{ cups} \end{array}$$

2 In January, 5,685 movie tickets were sold. The theater sold 183 more movie tickets in March than in January. How many tickets were sold in March?

3 Bill sold 127 boxes of Starblast candy and 839 packages of licorice. How many more packages of licorice than Starblast candy did Bill sell?

4 During the opening week of *Space Survivors,* the theater sold 1,386 tickets. The theater sold 884 tickets during the opening week of *Creatures from Orb.* How many more tickets were sold in the opening week of *Space Survivors*?

5 The ShowTime Theater has 1,253 seats. The Cinemania Theater has 784 seats. How many more seats does the ShowTime Theater have than the Cinemania Theater?

6 Lizzy sold 468 small buckets of popcorn, and Ted sold 245 large buckets of popcorn. How many buckets were sold altogether?

7 The ShowTime Theater has 962 tickets available for Monday night. They sell 543 tickets. How many tickets do they have left?

Name _____   Date_____

◇Start Here!

Solve each problem. The first problem is worked for you.

1 In Hawaii, the Kilauea volcano is 4,190 feet high. The Mount St. Helens volcano, located in Washington, is 8,364 feet high. How much higher is Mount St. Helens than Kilauea?

$$\begin{array}{r} \overset{2\ 1}{8,\cancel{3}64} \\ -\ 4,190 \\ \hline 4,174 \text{ feet} \end{array}$$

2 In the Caribbean Sea, the island of Barbados covers 166 square miles. The island of Jamaica measures 4,244 square miles. How many total square miles make up Barbados and Jamaica together?

3 The average depth of the Red Sea is 1,764 feet. The average depth of the Black Sea is 3,906 feet. How much deeper is the Black Sea than the Red Sea on average?

4 Castle Peak and Pikes Peak are both located in Colorado. Castle Peak is 14,265 feet high. Pikes Peak is 14,110. How much taller is Castle Peak?

5 The island of Hawaii measures 4,028 square miles. The island of Oahu is 600 square miles. How much larger is the island of Hawaii than Oahu?

6 Salt Lake City, Utah, has an altitude of 4,266 feet. Tulsa, Oklahoma, has an altitude of 804 feet. How much higher is Salt Lake City than Tulsa?

7 Lake Erie is 241 miles long. Lake Ontario is 193 miles long. How long are Lake Erie and Lake Ontario altogether?

Did you know?

One of the world's most active volcanoes is located in Hawaii. Kilauea has been erupting continuously since January 3, 1983. It has destroyed over 180 homes.

Name _____ Date_____

◇ **Start Here!**

Luzi's class took a poll at their school. They asked students what type of music they liked best. Use the results below to answer the questions that follow.

① How many students like pop music or country music?

```
  1 1 1
3,493
+ 1,998
5,491 students
```

Rosewood School's Favorite Music Poll

Rock	4,755 students
Pop	3,493 students
Country	1,998 students
Rap	1,043 students
Jazz	845 students
Oldies	391 students
Classical	173 students

② How many more students like rap music than jazz music?

③ How many students like oldies music or classical music?

④ More students like rock music than pop music. How many more students like rock music?

⑤ How many students like jazz music or oldies music?

⑥ How many more students like pop music than country music?

⑦ How many students like rock music or country music?

Name _____   Date_____

◇ Start Here!

Use the price list below to answer each question.

1 Eric's mom wants him to buy 1 gallon of milk and 3 boxes of cereal. How much money does he need?

$$\begin{array}{r} {}^{1\ 1}\\ \$2.89 \\ +\ \$10.79 \\ \hline \$13.68 \end{array}$$

Grocery List

1 bag of carrots	$1.79
1 package of grapes	$2.47
2 pounds of chicken	$6.62
1 gallon of milk	$2.89
3 loaves of bread	$3.58
8 cups of yogurt	$4.27
1 package of cheese	$5.59
3 boxes of cereal	$10.79
1 package of gum	$.76

2 Kendra buys 1 package of cheese. She pays for the cheese with a ten-dollar bill. How much change will Kendra get back?

3 Denzel buys 8 cups of yogurt and 3 loaves of bread. How much does Denzel spend altogether?

4 Kim has $15.25. She buys 2 pounds of chicken. How much does she have left?

5 Marc buys 1 package of grapes and 3 loaves of bread. His sister wants a package of gum. Marc only has $7.00 in his wallet. Does he have enough money to buy the gum?

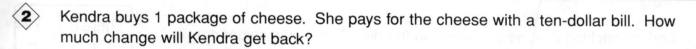

How much more does it cost to buy 1 package of grapes than to buy 1 bag of carrots?

6

7 Maggie buys 3 loaves of bread. She pays for her purchase with a five-dollar bill. How much change does she get back?

8 Gary buys 2 pounds of chicken and 3 boxes of cereal. How much money does Gary spend altogether?

Name _____   Date_____

◇ **Start Here!**

Lori is on a safari to observe animals. She's keeping a diary of the things she sees. Help her finish writing about what she saw.

1 Lori sees 3 times as many giraffes as elephants. Lori sees 6 elephants. How many giraffes does Lori see?

$$\begin{array}{r} 3 \\ \underline{\times\ 6} \\ 18 \quad \textbf{giraffes} \end{array}$$

2 Lori and her group travel in jeeps while looking at the animals. Each jeep has 4 seats. There are 7 jeeps in the group. How many people are in Lori's group if all of the seats are filled?

3 Lori is watching 2 spiders crawling in the dirt. The brown spider crawls twice as far as the black spider. The black spider crawls 3 feet. How far does the brown spider crawl?

There's a lot of math on a safari!

4 Each day, Lori drinks 3 bottles of water. How many bottles of water will Lori drink in a week?

5 Lori sees 4 herds of wildebeest. Each herd has 9 wildebeest. How many wildebeest does Lori see?

6 In the evening, Lori helps set up camp. There are 3 rows with 8 tents in each row. How many tents are there?

Did you know?
A cheetah can run twice as fast as a giraffe. The cheetah can run up to 70 miles per hour.

www.summerbridgeactivities.com

Lots of Cars

Name _____ Date_____

◇ Start Here!

Solve each problem. The first problem is worked for you.

1 Jasmine is buying a sports car. There are 3 rows of sports cars with 7 cars in each row. How many sports cars are there in all?

$$
\begin{array}{r}
3 \\
\underline{\times 7} \\
21 \quad \text{sports cars}
\end{array}
$$

2 Each car has 4 tires. There are 9 cars. How many tires are there altogether?

3 Morgan wants to test drive a car and needs the key. Each key ring has 6 keys. If there are 9 key rings, how many keys are there total?

4 Chloe wants a new truck. The car dealer has 7 times as many trucks as cars. The car dealer has 8 cars. How many trucks does the car dealer have?

5 Sara likes red cars. The Motor Madness car lot has 5 times as many red cars as the Speeds-a-Lot car lot. The Speeds-a-Lot car lot has 8 red cars. How many red cars are on the Motor Madness car lot?

6 Jason sees 4 times as many sport utility vehicles as sports cars. Jason sees 3 sports cars. How many sport utility vehicles does Jason see?

7 Gina test drove the red car 3 times as many miles as she drove the blue car. Gina test drove the blue car 7 miles. How many miles did Gina drive the red car?

8 Stan uses 2 bottles of car polish on his car every month. How many bottles of car polish will Stan use in 9 months?

Name _____   Date_____

◇ Start Here!

Solve each problem using the prices below. Remember to put the "$" sign in your answer.

1 Lisa buys a soda and the markers. How much does she spend?

$$\begin{array}{r} \overset{1}{\$1.25} \\ +\ \$6.45 \\ \hline \$7.70 \end{array}$$

soda	$ 1.25
comic book	$ 3.75
pretzel	$ 2.36
T-shirt	$ 5.27
candy	$ 2.65
markers	$ 6.45
socks	$ 7.50
CD	$14.87

2 How much more does the comic book cost than the candy?

3 Jason has $10.00. If he buys a T-shirt, how much money will he have left?

4 How much will Emily spend if she buys socks and a pretzel?

5 Henry wants a new comic book, but he only has $1.63. How much more money does Henry need to buy the comic book?

6 Abby gets hungry and buys a soda and a pretzel. How much money does she spend on food?

7 Kurt has $17.75. He decides to buy some new socks because all of his socks have holes in them. Does he have enough money left over to buy the markers?

www.summerbridgeactivities.com

Name _____ Date_____

◇ **Start Here!**

Solve each problem using the prices below.

---

1. Leslie buys a soda and a hurricane hot dog. How much does
she spend? Leslie pays for her
dinner with a ten-dollar bill. How
much change will she get back?

	soda	$1.49
	native nachos	$4.75
	jungle burger	$3.49
	fries	$2.39

Home of the Jungle Burger!

hurricane hot dog	$ 3.55
tropical twist shake	$ 3.75
crunch 'n munch meal	$28.55

TRY IT!

Crunch 'N Munch Meal

$$\begin{array}{r} \overset{1\ 1}{} \\ \$1.49 \\ +\ \$3.55 \\ \hline \$5.04 \end{array} \qquad \begin{array}{r} \overset{9\ 9\ 1}{\$\cancel{10.00}} \\ -\ \$5.04 \\ \hline \$4.96 \end{array}$$

---

2. Eric has $15.00. If he buys the native nachos and a tropical twist shake, how much
money will he have left?

3. How much will Ashaki spend if she buys a jungle burger and a soda?

4. Sam's family orders a crunch 'n munch meal. Sam orders a tropical twist shake.
Sam's mom only has $30.00. How much more money will Sam need to give his mom
so she can pay for the family's dinner?

5. How much more does the hurricane hot dog cost than the jungle burger?

6. Webster has $8.00. He buys a jungle burger and fries. The fries are salty, and he
decides he wants a soda. How much money will Webster have left if he buys a soda?

7. Lisa buys a soda and fries. She pays for her dinner with a five-dollar bill.
How much change should Lisa get back?

Name _____   Date_____

◇ Start Here!

Emmett is helping his brother in the pet store after school. Help him find the answer to each problem.

1 Emmett is going to feed the rabbits. There are 11 cages with 4 rabbits in each cage. How many rabbits will Emmett need to feed?

$$\begin{array}{r} 11 \\ \underline{\times\ 4} \\ \textbf{44 rabbits} \end{array}$$

---

2 The pet store sells 2 times as many red pet collars as blue pet collars. Emmett sells 42 blue pet collars. How many red pet collars does Emmett sell?

3 There are 21 turtles. Emmett feeds 2 lettuce leaves to each turtle. How many lettuce leaves does it take to feed all of the turtles?

4 Emmett helps take the dogs for a walk. There are 3 times as many poodles as cocker spaniels. There are 13 cocker spaniels. How many poodles are there?

5 Emmett is ordering more canary seed for the pet store. If the canaries eat 4 bags of seed in a month, how many bags will Emmett need to order for the next 12 months?

6 The iguanas eat 3 times a week. How many times will Emmett need to feed the iguanas in the next 32 weeks?

7 Emmett sells 3 times as many dog toys as cat toys. Emmett sells 23 cat toys. How many dog toys does Emmett sell?

Did you know?

While a cat is sleeping, its body temperature drops slightly. This explains why some cats like to sleep next to their owner or in the sunlight where it is warmer.

Iguanas have a third eye located on the top of their head. The third eye is called a parietal eye. It can detect light and darkness, but not colored things.

Name _____ Date_____

◇ **Start Here!**

Solve each problem. The first problem is worked for you.

1 Max needs 48 pounds of grass seed for each lawn he plants. If Max plants 3 lawns, how many pounds of grass seed will he need?

2

48

x 3

144 pounds of grass seed

2 Spencer is planting tomato plants. There are 5 rows of 47 tomato plants. How many tomato plants did Spencer plant altogether?

3 Lizzie has 17 watering cans. Each watering can holds 6 gallons of water. How many gallons of water will it take to fill all 17 watering cans?

4 Jess is putting fertilizer on 23 lawns. He needs 4 bags of fertilizer for each lawn. How many bags of fertilizer will Jess need to buy?

5 Sara is mowing lawns for the summer. She mows 5 lawns a week. If Sara mows lawns for 23 weeks, how many lawns will she mow altogether?

6 Kaleb has 3 times as many garden tools as Anne. Anne has 37 garden tools. How many garden tools does Kaleb have?

7 Josh plants 59 squash plants. Each plant has 6 squash growing on the vine. How many squash does Josh have?

8 Kim's sunflower grew 5 times as high as Ryan's sunflower. Ryan's sunflower is 13 inches tall. How tall is Kim's sunflower?

I'm growing a row of numbers.

Bookworm Bonanza

Name _____ Date_____

◇ Start Here!

Solve each problem. The first problem is worked for you.

1 Hillary reads 842 pages a week. How many pages will Hillary read in 9 weeks?

$$\begin{array}{r} \overset{3\ 1}{842} \\ \underline{\times\ 9} \\ 7{,}578 \text{ pages} \end{array}$$

2 Each day, 328 people come to the library. How many people will come to the library in a week?

3 Each magazine box holds 9 magazines. The library has 528 full magazine boxes. How many magazines does the library have?

4 Gary checked out 467 books in a year. Kristen checked out 3 times as many books as Gary. How many books did Kristen check out?

5 The Southtown Library has 8 times as many books as the Littleton Library. The Littleton Library has 356 books. How many books does the Southtown Library have?

6 There are 8 bookshelves on aisle A. Each bookshelf has 295 books on it. How many books are on aisle A?

7 Russell read 4 times as many pages as Beth. Beth read 765 pages. How many pages did Russell read?

8 The Northtown Library has 4 times as many novels as biographies. The Northtown Library has 274 biographies. How many novels does the Northtown Library have?

Did you know?
In the year 2000, a total of 23.3 million Harry Potter books were sold in the United States.

Name _____   Date_____

◇ **Start Here!**

Solve each problem. The first problem is worked for you.

1 Max has $8.32 in his pocket. What coins and bills could Max have?

1 five-dollar bill, 3 one-dollar bills, 1 quarter, 1 nickel, and 2 pennies

---

2 Tia has 3 one-dollar bills, 2 quarters, and 1 dime in her piggy bank. How much money does Tia have?

3 Mr. Cardoza is buying doughnuts for his class. The doughnuts cost $13.49. He has 1 ten-dollar bill, 3 one-dollar bills, and 2 quarters in his wallet. Does he have enough money to pay for the doughnuts?

4 Lance has 2 five-dollar bills, 4 dimes, and 2 nickels in his wallet. How much money does Lance have altogether?

5 Sheena has $11.76 in her bank. What coins and bills could Sheena have?

6 Penny has 3 ten-dollar bills, 3 quarters, and 5 nickels. How much money does she have?

7 Jackson has 2 one-dollar bills, 8 dimes, and 3 pennies in his pocket. How much money does Jackson have total?

8 Annie needs $8.75 to buy her school supplies. She has 1 five-dollar bill, 3 one-dollar bills, 2 quarters, and a dime in her purse. Does she have enough money to buy her school supplies?

9 Caroline has $17.43 in her bank. What coins and bills could Caroline have?

Crazy Carnival

Name _____ Date_____

◇ **Start Here!**

Solve each problem. The first problem is worked for you.

1 Isabella buys 9 balloons for 35¢ each. How much does she spend in all?

$$\begin{array}{r}4\\35\\\times 9\\\hline 315\end{array}$$ ¢

2 Tyler, Ann, and Jason want to get their faces painted. Face painting costs 69¢. How much money will the 3 of them need to have their faces painted?

3 Carl buys 256 tickets for 3¢ each. How much does he spend on tickets?

4 Charlotte rides the Spin-a-Whirl 19 times. If 1 ride costs 5¢, how much does Charlotte spend on Spin-a-Whirl rides altogether?

5 Jess buys 146 pieces of candy for 6¢ each. How much does he spend in all?

6 T-shirts cost $18 each. Amy buys 7 T-shirts. How much does Amy spend on T-shirts?

7 Nick buys 5 slices of pizza. Each slice of pizza costs 89¢. How much does Nick spend on pizza?

8 At the toss-a-ring game, each ring costs 3¢. Erin buys 76 rings. How much does she spend?

9 Enrica has 9 friends. She buys each friend a soda for 79¢ each. How much does she spend on sodas?

Name _____ Date_____

◇ Start Here!

Solve each problem. The first problem is worked for you.

1 Jonathan delivers 9 newspapers. He gets paid $1.14 for each newspaper he delivers. How much money does Jonathan earn?

$$\begin{array}{r} \overset{1\quad 3}{\$1.14} \\ \underline{\times\ 9} \\ \$10.26 \end{array}$$

2 Annie places an ad in the newspaper. The newspaper charges 5¢ a word. Annie's ad has 694 words. How much does the ad cost Annie?

3 Desi spends $34.56 at the newsstand. Meg spends $58.31 at the newsstand. How much more money did Meg spend than Desi?

4 The *Daily Times* sells 491 newspapers for 4¢ each. How much money does the *Daily Times* make?

5 Tara buys 2 newspapers that cost $3.95 each. She gives the clerk $10.00. How much change does Tara get back?

6 The *Globe* sells 938 newspapers for 3¢ each. The *Tribune* sells 443 newspapers for 6¢ each. How much money does each newspaper make? Which newspaper company makes more money?

7 James buys 4 newspapers for $5.34 each. He also buys a special edition newspaper for $1.79. How much money does James spend altogether?

8 Belle gets paid 9¢ for each word she writes. Belle writes 4,593 words. How much money does Belle earn?

© Rainbow Bridge Publishing

Math Word Problems—Grade 3—RBP3640

Name _____   Date_____

◇ **Start Here!**

Chloe and her family are taking a vacation. Help her solve the following problems.

1   Chloe's family waits for her brother to get home. It's 6:00, and they wait for 30 minutes. What time is it now?

6:30

2   Chloe's family leaves at 7:15. They drive for 30 minutes and then stop for dinner. What time is it when they stop for dinner?

3   At 8:45 Chloe asks how much longer it will take to get to their hotel. Her mom says it will take 1 hour and 30 minutes more. What time will they reach their hotel?

4   At 9:00 Chloe's little brother needs to stop for a break. The family stops for 15 minutes. What time do they get back on the road again?

5   Chloe sets her alarm clock for 7:15 in the morning. She oversleeps 30 minutes. What time does Chloe get up?

6   Chloe is excited to get to the amusement park. The family reaches the amusement park at 8:00. They wait in line to get in for 45 minutes. What time is it when they go inside the park?

Name _____ Date_____

◇ Start Here!

Solve each problem. The first problem is worked for you.

1 Henry, Misha, and Ann buy a package of licorice. There are 12 pieces of licorice in the package. How many pieces will each person get?

$$12 \div 3 = 4 \text{ pieces of licorice}$$

---

2 Jason divides 36 pieces of bubble gum among 4 friends. How many pieces of bubble gum will each person get?

3 The jar of jawbreakers has 20 pieces. Four customers buy equal numbers of jawbreakers until the jar is empty. How many pieces did each customer buy?

4 A case of candy bars contains 72 bars. There are 9 boxes in a case. How many candy bars are in each box?

5 Dotty, Jackson, and Susan share a package of gumdrops equally. If the package contains 18 gumdrops, how many will each person get?

6 Mason gives 42 packages of Tart-n-Tangies to 7 friends to share equally. How many packages of Tart-n-Tangies do each of his friends get?

7 Nine jelly beans fit into a container. Amber has 72 jelly beans. How many containers does she need?

8 April buys a package of gum and divides it equally with her sister. If there are 12 pieces of gum in the package, how many pieces will each girl get?

Candy, candy!

Name _____   Date_____

◇Start Here!

Solve each problem. The first problem is worked for you.

1 Camp Oakwood has 120 campers. If there are 5 campers in each tent, how many tents are there?

120 ÷ 5 = 24 tents

2 Megan has a package of 376 marshmallows. If each camper roasts 8 marshmallows, how many campers can roast marshmallows?

3 Dave has a case of 228 flashlights. There are 3 boxes in a case. How many flashlights are in each box?

4 Tim made 588 sandwiches for the campers in 1 week. How many sandwiches did Tim make each day?

5 Robin has 365 packages of trail mix. She puts 5 packages in each backpack. How many backpacks does she fill?

6 Kendra has 276 inches of string. She cuts the string into 6-inch pieces for making bracelets. How many 6-inch pieces of string can she cut?

7 Shannon has 585 gallons of punch. If the campers use 9 gallons of punch per day, how many days will the punch last?

8 Camp Hillcrest has 189 campers. If 7 sleeping bags fit in 1 tent, how many tents will Camp Hillcrest need?

9 Rob cooked 108 strips of bacon. Each camper ate 3 strips of bacon. How many campers ate bacon?

Name _____   Date_____

◇ Start Here!

Solve each problem. The first problem is worked for you.

1 Samantha bakes 252 cupcakes for her birthday party. She gives each guest a box with 4 cupcakes. How many boxes does she have?

$$252 \div 4 = 63 \text{ boxes}$$

2 Jill buys 349 party favors for 7¢ each. How much does Jill spend?

3 Bill has 72 cans of soda in 6-packs. How many 6-packs does he have?

4 A bunch of 12 balloons costs $13.99. If Marissa buys 3 bunches, how much does she spend on balloons?

5 Vivian has 396 party hats. Each package contains 6 party hats. How many packages of party hats does Vivian have?

6 Amanda puts up decorations. She has 224 inches of ribbon and needs to cut 7-inch pieces. How many 7-inch pieces can she cut?

Everyone is invited to my birthday party!

7 Carter brings 3 cakes. Each cake has 18 pieces. If there are 60 guests, will Carter have enough pieces? If not, how many more will he need?

8 Sean has 4 times as many guests at his party as Alex. Alex has 53 guests at his party. How many guests does Sean have?

9 Each person that came to Eric's party brought 3 gifts. Eric had 23 people come to his party. How many gifts did Eric get?

© Rainbow Bridge Publishing

Name _____ Date_____

◇ Start Here!

Color in the correct parts that are used for each fraction. Then write the fraction.

1   Jada cut the pie into 6 pieces. Jada and her friends ate 3 pieces.

Remember…
The TOP part of the fraction
tells how many parts you USE.

The BOTTOM part of the fraction
tells how many parts there are.

$$\frac{3}{6}$$

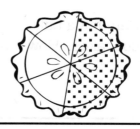

2   Brendon had 12 stickers. He gave 7 stickers to his friends.

3   The pepperoni pizza has 6 slices. Alex eats 4 slices.

4   Randy has 8 marbles. He loses 5 of the marbles when they roll down a crack in the sidewalk.

5   Karen has 9 chocolate kisses. She gives 6 chocolate kisses to her mom.

6   The pet store has 7 animals, and 2 of the animals are dogs.

7   The cookie jar has 4 cookies. Mallory eats 1 cookie.

Pizza Party

Name _____ Date_____

◇ Start Here!

Rob and his friends are making pizzas for their party. Help them solve the following problems.

1 First, Rob puts 3/4 cup of flour in a bowl for the pizza dough. Then he adds another 1/4 cup of flour. How much flour did he put in the dough?

3/4 + 1/4 = 4/4 or 1 cup of flour

2 Marcy rolls out the pizza dough. She uses 1/2 cup. Then she adds another 1/2 cup to make the pizza larger. How many cups did she use altogether?

3 Jan chops 1/3 cup of mushrooms. She likes mushrooms, so she chops another 2/3 cup. How many cups of mushrooms did she chop?

4 Lexie puts 3/6 tablespoon of tomato sauce on the pizza. Then she adds 2/6 tablespoon of tomato sauce. How much tomato sauce did she put on the pizza altogether?

5 John grates 3/8 cup of cheese. Then he grates another 4/8 cup of cheese. How much cheese did John grate altogether?

6 Jan puts 2/16 cup of pepperoni on the pizza. Then she adds another 8/16 cup of pepperoni. How much pepperoni is on the pizza?

> Anyone ready for 1/16 of a pizza?

7 Marcy adds 1/6 teaspoon of pepper. Then she adds 4/6 teaspoon of pepper. How much pepper did she use on the pizza?

8 The pizza is finally done, and Rob and his friends are going to eat. Rob eats 9/16 of the pizza, and John eats 7/16 of the pizza. How much did Rob and John eat altogether? How much pizza is left for the rest of their friends?

Name _____ Date_____

◇**Start Here!**

Solve each problem. The first problem is worked for you.

1 Beth sees some ants crawling toward her picnic basket. 9/16 of the ants are black. 7/16 of the ants are red. How many more black ants are there than red ants?

9/16 – 7/16 = 2/16 black ants

---

2 In the park, 3/5 of the trees were elm trees. 2/5 of the trees were oak trees. How many more elm trees than oak trees were there in the park?

3 Les had 8/8 of a bottle of soda. He drank 4/8 of the bottle. How much does Les have left?

4 Jasmine runs 3/4 of a mile. Dan runs 1/4 of a mile less than Jasmine. How far does Dan run?

5 Alex watches kites flying. 7/16 of the kites are red, and 9/16 of the kites are blue. How many more blue kites than red kites are there?

6 Max and Darla fly their kites. Max's kite flies 5/4 of a yard. Darla's kite flies 2/4 of a yard less than Max's kite. How many yards did Darla's kite fly?

7 Adam brings 2/3 of a pound of candy to the park. He shares 1/3 of a pound of candy with his friends. How much candy does he have left?

8 Kevin and Sara go skating. Kevin skates 9/10 of a mile. Sara skates 2/10 of a mile less than Kevin. How far does Sara skate?

Name _____ Date_____

◇ Start Here!

Solve each problem. The first problem is worked for you.

1 Rich bought 5/16 quart of white paint and 11/16 quart of blue paint. How much more blue paint did Rich buy?

11/16 − 5/16 = 6/16 quart

2 Heidi bought a gallon of paint. She needs 3/4 of a gallon to paint her garage door. She spills 2/4 of a gallon of paint. How much more paint does Heidi need to buy so she will have enough?

3 Mitch mixes 6/8 of a quart of pink paint with 1/8 of a quart of white paint. How much paint does he end up with?

4 Maria is at the paint store buying paintbrushes. 7/10 of the paintbrushes are large, and 3/10 of the paintbrushes are small. How many more large paintbrushes than small paintbrushes are there?

5 Daisy needs 8/12 of a quart of paint to paint her backyard fence. She buys 1 quart of paint at the paint store. How much paint will Daisy have left?

My favorite color is purple!

6 Gary is painting his new doghouse. He uses 5/16 of a can of red paint on the sides of the house and 4/16 of a can of black paint for the roof. How much paint does Gary use on the doghouse altogether?

7 Lisa uses 3/9 of a gallon of paint in her bathroom. She uses 5/9 of a gallon in her bedroom. How much paint does Lisa use in both her bathroom and bedroom?

Name _____ Date_____

◇**Start Here!**

Answer the following questions using the graphs below.

Third-Grade Students' Favorite Popsicle™ Flavors

This is a pie chart. It shows the favorite flavors
of Popsicles for the third graders at
Viewmont Elementary School.

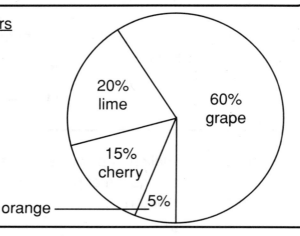

20%
lime

60%
grape

15%
cherry

5%

orange ————

1) What is the favorite flavor of Popsicle for
third grade students? **grape**

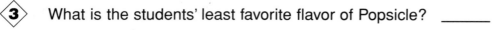

2) How many more students like grape Popsicles more than orange Popsicles? _____

3) What is the students' least favorite flavor of Popsicle? _____

4) What percent of students like cherry or lime Popsicles? _____

Points Scored at the Playoff Game

This is a bar graph. There is one bar for each person.
Taisha and her friends played in the playoff basketball
game for their school. The graph shows how many
points they earned for their team.

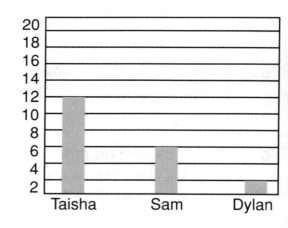

20
18
16
14
12
10
8
6
4
2

Taisha   Sam   Dylan

1) How many points did Sam score? _____

2) How many more points did Taisha score than Dylan? _____

3) How many points did Sam, Taisha, and Dylan score altogether? _____

4) How many points are represented by each line on the bar graph? _____

Name _____   Date_____

◇ **Start Here!**

Allie asked each class member what type of pet he or she has. Record the results on the bar graph below.

Type of Pet	Number of Students
Dog	9
Goldfish	7
Cat	6
Lizard	3
No Pet	2
Turtle	1

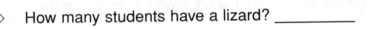

Use the bar graph to answer the questions.

◇1   What type of pet do the most students in the class have? **dog**

◇2   How many students have a lizard? _____

◇3   What is the least popular pet in the class? _____

The chart below shows the number of items sold at Sporty's Sporting Goods store. Put the information in a bar graph.

Item	Number Sold
Basketballs	18
Tennis Rackets	15
Baseballs	12
Bats	12
Gloves	6

Use the bar graph to answer the questions.

◇1   How many tennis rackets were sold? _____

◇2   Which two items had equal numbers sold? _____ _____

◇3   How many more basketballs than baseballs were sold? _____

                         Math Word Problems—Grade 3—RBP3640

Name _____ Date_____

◇ Start Here!

Solve each problem. The first problem is worked for you.

1   Meg sold 397 tickets at the fair. Sam sold 5 times as many tickets as Meg. How many tickets did Sam sell?

$$
\begin{array}{r}
{}^{4\,3}\\
397\\
\times\ 5\\
\hline
1{,}985 \quad \text{tickets}
\end{array}
$$

2   There were 69 jars of pickles at the pickle judging contest. Each jar had 9 pickles in it. How many pickles were there altogether?

3   The state fair is open for 9 weeks. How many days is that?

4   Mitch buys a soda for $1.45 and a hamburger for $3.54. He pays with a ten-dollar bill. How much change does Mitch get back?

5   The Twist-a-Whirl has 15 cars. Each car holds 4 people. How many people can ride the Twist-a-Whirl at a time?

6   Janice sold 7 times as many packages of cotton candy as Tim. Tim sold 295 packages of cotton candy. How many packages of cotton candy did Janice sell?

7   The fair closes at 10:45. Karen checks her watch at 9:15 to see if she has time to ride the Ferris wheel. How much time does Karen have left before the fair closes?

8   Andre buys a toy car for $7.32 and a T-shirt for $15.39. How much money does Andre spend altogether?

9   The kiddie coaster holds 28 people. If 2 people can ride in a car, how many cars are there?

Answer Pages

Page 3
1. 18 goldfish
2. 26 fewer guppies
3. 120 goldfish
4. 14 plants
5. 86 goldfish
6. 58 more comets
7. 42 guppies

Page 4
Answers will vary.

Page 5
1. 18° F
2. 18 inches
3. 27° F
4. 15 miles per hour
5. 19° F

Page 6
1. 2,096 cups
2. 5,868 tickets
3. 712 packages
4. 502 tickets
5. 469 seats
6. 713 buckets
7. 419 tickets

Page 7
1. 4,174 feet
2. 4,410 square miles
3. 2,142 feet
4. 155 feet
5. 3,428 square miles
6. 3,462 feet
7. 434 miles long

Page 8
1. 5,491 students
2. 198 students
3. 564 students
4. 1,262 students
5. 1,236 students
6. 1,495 students
7. 6,753 students

Page 9
1. $13.68
2. $4.41
3. $7.85
4. $8.63
5. Yes, he has $6.05 left.
6. $0.68
7. $1.42
8. $17.41

Page 10
1. 18 giraffes
2. 28 people
3. 6 feet
4. 21 bottles of water
5. 36 wildebeest
6. 24 tents

Page 11
1. 21 sports cars
2. 36 tires
3. 54 keys
4. 56 trucks
5. 40 red cars
6. 12 sport utility vehicles
7. 21 miles
8. 18 bottles

Page 12
1. $7.70
2. $1.10
3. $4.73
4. $9.86
5. $2.12
6. $3.61
7. Yes, he has $10.25 left.

Page 13
1. $5.04, $4.96
2. $6.50
3. $4.98
4. $2.30
5. $0.06
6. $0.63
7. $1.12

Page 14
1. 44 rabbits
2. 84 red pet collars
3. 42 lettuce leaves
4. 39 poodles
5. 48 bags of seed
6. 96 times
7. 69 dog toys

Page 15
1. 144 pounds of grass seed
2. 235 tomato plants
3. 102 gallons
4. 92 bags of fertilizer
5. 115 lawns
6. 111 garden tools
7. 354 squash
8. 65 inches

Page 16
1. 7,578 pages
2. 2,296 people
3. 4,752 magazines
4. 1,401 books
5. 2,848 books
6. 2,360 books
7. 3,060 pages
8. 1,096 novels

Page 17
1. (Answers will vary.) 1 five-dollar bill, 3 one-dollar bills,
   1 quarter, 1 nickel and 2 pennies
2. $3.60
3. Yes, he has $13.50.
4. $10.50
5. (Answers will vary.) 1 ten-dollar bill, 1 one-dollar bill, 3 quarters
   and 1 penny
6. $31.00
7. $2.83
8. No, she only has $8.60.
9. (Answers will vary.) 1 ten-dollar bill, 1 five-dollar bill,
   2 one-dollar bills, 1 quarter, 1 dime, 1 nickel and 3 pennies

Page 18
1. 315¢ or $3.15
2. 207¢ or $2.07
3. 768¢ or $7.68
4. 95¢ or $0.95
5. 876¢ or $8.76
6. $126
7. 445¢ or $4.45
8. 228¢ or $2.28
9. 711¢ or $7.11

Page 19
1. $10.26
2. 3,470¢ or $34.70
3. $23.75
4. 1,964¢ or $19.64
5. $2.10
6. The *Globe* makes 2,814¢ or $28.14, and the
   Tribune makes 2,658¢ or $26.58.
   The *Globe* makes more money.
7. $23.15
8. 41,337¢ or $413.37

Page 20
1. 6:30
2. 7:45
3. 10:15
4. 9:15
5. 7:45
6. 8:45

© Rainbow Bridge Publishing

Math Word Problems—Grade 3—RBP3640

Answer Pages

Page 21
1. 4 pieces of licorice
2. 9 pieces of bubble gum
3. 5 pieces
4. 8 candy bars
5. 6 gumdrops
6. 6 packages of Tart-n-Tangies
7. 8 containers
8. 6 pieces of gum

Page 22
1. 24 tents
2. 47 campers
3. 76 flashlights
4. 84 sandwiches
5. 73 backpacks
6. 46 pieces of string
7. 65 days
8. 27 tents
9. 36 campers

Page 23
1. 63 boxes
2. 2,443¢ or $24.43
3. 12 6-packs
4. $41.97
5. 66 packages
6. 32 pieces of ribbon
7. He has 54 pieces, so he will need 6 more pieces.
8. 212 guests
9. 69 gifts

Page 24
1. 3/6

2. 7/12

3. 4/6

4. 5/8

5. 6/9

6. 2/7

7. 1/4

Page 25
1. 4/4 or 1 cup
2. 2/2 or 1 cup
3. 3/3 or 1 cup
4. 5/6 tablespoon
5. 7/8 cup
6. 10/16 cup
7. 5/6 teaspoon
8. 16/16 or 1 whole; no pizza is left

Page 26
1. 2/16 black ants
2. 1/5 more elm trees
3. 4/8 of a bottle
4. 2/4 of a mile
5. 2/16 more blue kites
6. 3/4 of a yard
7. 1/3 of a pound
8. 7/10 of a mile

Page 27
1. 6/16 quart
2. 1/4 gallon
3. 7/8 quart
4. 4/10 more large paintbrushes
5. 4/12 quart
6. 9/16 can
7. 8/9 gallon

Page 28
1. grape
2. 55%
3. orange
4. 35%

1. 6 points
2. 10 points
3. 20 points
4. 2 points

Page 29
1. dog
2. 3 students
3. turtle

1. 15 tennis rackets
2. baseballs and bats
3. 6 more basketballs

Page 30
1. 41,985 tickets
2. 621 pickles
3. 63 days
4. $5.01
5. 60 people
6. 2,065 packages
7. 1 hour and 30 minutes
8. $22.71
9. 14 cars